The Art of the Mandala

Adrienne Burke

STERLING INNOVATION
An imprint of Sterling Publishing Co., Inc.

New York / London
www.sterlingpublishing.com

STERLING and the distinctive Sterling logo are registered trademarks of
Sterling Publishing Co., Inc.

Library of Congress Cataloging-in-Publication Data Available

2 4 6 8 10 9 7 5 3

Produced by LightSpeed Publishing, Inc. and X-Height Studio
Mandala illustrations by Jeffrey Calafato and Gwendolyn DeRungs

Published by Sterling Publishing Co., Inc.
387 Park Avenue South, New York, NY 10016
© 2007 by Sterling Publishing Co., Inc.
Distributed in Canada by Sterling Publishing
c/o Canadian Manda Group, 165 Dufferin Street
Toronto, Ontario, Canada M6K 3H6
Distributed in the United Kingdom by GMC Distribution Services
Castle Place, 166 High Street, Lewes, East Sussex, England BN7 1XU
Distributed in Australia by Capricorn Link (Australia) Pty. Ltd.
P.O. Box 704, Windsor, NSW 2756, Australia

Printed in China

Sterling ISBN-13: 978-1-4027-5722-8
ISBN-10: 1-4027-5722-0

For information about custom editions, special sales, premium and
corporate purchases, please contact Sterling Special Sales
Department at 800-805-5489 or specialsales@sterlingpublishing.com.

Table of Contents

What Is a Mandala?

A BUDDHIST MONK IN A saffron robe is creating a mandala of millions of brilliantly colored grains of sand. He holds a metal funnel called a chak-pur in one hand while rubbing a metal rod over its grated surface; the vibration causes the sand to flow like liquid. We have all played with sand as children, but this art is not the ordinary sand castle.

The mandala is round, a circle, a disc, an orb, a ring, a ball, a wheel, a halo, a mark, a territory, a labyrinth, a district, a province, a neighborhood, a group, the center, a collection, a whole body, a society, a community, a connection. All of these words are definitions of the Sanskrit word *mandala*. The word itself is derived from the root word *manda*, which means essence. The suffix *la* can mean container. So it can be said that a mandala is the pure essence. A mandala is a tool or a way of discovery. It is a mirror that reflects the evolution of our inner processes and how they manifest in the outer world.

It is a visual symbol of a man or woman and how each is an individual and also a part of the world at large.

Through its imagery it shows the mind, the body, and the divine. It is a representation of how the microcosm is as important as the macrocosm and how each is interdependent upon the other. A mandala is a communication of how the individual soul is an integral part of the entire universe. It draws our attention inward and enables us to understand its symbolic meaning and absorb this into the mind. It is through the conception, creation, application, and study of the mandala that one receives its message. It is a message unique to each person. The patterns can be found in nature and are seen in biology, geometry, geology, chemistry, physics, and astronomy. Our solar system is a metaphor that is often used to represent the workings of the mandala. The sun is the center or hub, and the planets rotate around the solar sphere. The sun gives light, warmth, and life. Without the sun the planets would not exist; there would be no life. Yet if there were no planets, the sun would have no reason to exist. Each is co-dependent on the other. It is hard to say whether the sun came first and the planets second, or if it is because of the planets that there is a sun. It is so with a mandala. There is a focal point but it is part of whole.

Mandalas can be used to serve numerous needs. Some people use the mandala as a divination tool, a way to focus their mind in order to see clearly. Others use it to unblock negative energy patterns, as a means of observation and healing. Others use it as a way to analyze the mind by objectively dissecting the patterns and symbols created in the art. Others use it as an offering to get closer to the divine, and still others use it as a form of self-expression. A mandala can be designed by instinct and intuition—going with the creative flow. Or a mandala can be an intense and highly concentrated mental process.

History of the Mandala

The mandala is an ancient religious symbol found in many cultures. It is usually a complex, circular design, divided into four or eight parts. The design leads the eye around the circle, allowing the viewer to discover new areas, and it eventually draws the eye to the center.

Mandalas are said to have originated thousands of years ago, before the time of Christ. Some even say there were mandalas before civilization began. Early mandalas can be found in cave drawings and rock inscriptions created by our ancestors, as a reflection of spiritual energy. Mandalas were first mentioned in the Rig Veda, the most ancient Hindu Scripture dated 1700-1100 BCE. Rig Veda means "sacred knowledge of hymns and praise." The Vedas were said to be divined and compiled by the Rishis or seers who were given the words from the gods.

The Rig Veda is organized into ten group patterns known as mandalas. These patterns describe a lifestyle towards prosperous and righteous living—a way to be in tune with the cosmos or the gods. This scripture details disciplines leading to realization of the absolute. It is through these words that the mandala of form was born.

The mandala we think about is a circular art form that at one point was only practiced by monks. However, the circular shape is one of the oldest forms of art created by human beings. The first shape a child draws is most frequently a circle. Some say the formation of the rocks of Stonehenge form a mandala. Crop circles, besides being mysterious, are mandalas as well. We see mandalas everywhere, from ancient art and architecture to today's modern designs. Cities of long ago were built in circular structures. Think of the ancient city of Rome. The hub of the city was where all the commerce and politics or legislation took place. The outskirts of the hub (or downtown, if you will) are where people lived, and further out still is where agriculture and manufacturing occurred.

Mandalas represent the flow of existence—a beginning, a middle, and an end, which leads to another beginning. The smallest atom is a mandala as is an area as vast as our solar system.

Why Mandalas Are Used

Mandalas traditionally have been used in concentration and meditation practice. The individual first creates the design of the mandala, which can incorporate pictures of deities and story lines, as well as various shapes, symbols, and colors. It is through this creation process that the mind becomes so focused that it turns off its normal chatter. The individual begins to merge the mind to the process, thus training it to be still. The conscious mind uses words to categorize and define our experiences. The unconscious mind deals in images and symbols, which give us various perceptions.

The nature of the mind is to wander and to think—to create ongoing chatter or dialogue. But with all the noise, it is hard to be clear-headed. In the east it is said that the mind is like a baby monkey, running and jumping here and there, but never settling down, never stopping. Through the process of continual focus and refocus, and refocus yet again, the monkey settles down. It may be hard to understand this metaphor in the west since we do not normally see monkeys, but try to replace the idea of the monkey with a puppy. When we get new puppies, they are very happy. They eagerly explore and get into everything. They are always going. In order to train a puppy you need repetition, patience, and discipline. As soon as they stop for a moment, they jump up to lick your face. So you repeat and repeat and repeat again. It is the same with the mind. Quietly the mind takes a method. When you tune into a mandala with strong concentration and devoted practice, you can experience a change in consciousness.

Mandalas should always be unique; they are a representation of the person who is creating them and that person's intention. Usually a mandala is made for a specific purpose, for example, a mandala devoted to world peace. Traditionally mandalas are made while the artist or artists are meditating or praying. This is done to increase the energy of the devotion.

Mandalas are representations of focus and the ability to change. They allow the person who is creating them to put a process behind a concept. In some Tibetan Buddhist traditions, mandalas are used in rituals of initiation. They are constructed at the beginning of the initiation, out of grains of colored sand, shells, stones, or even crushed gemstones carefully placed on a specially prepared platform. At the end of the initiation, the mandalas are deliberately destroyed. Days or weeks of work are ruined in a few minutes. But the monks do not see their creation as ruined or finished, rather they see it as a reminder or a message. It shows the impermanence of today and how the only constant in our lives is change.

Different Cultures
and Mandalas

THE MANDALA CAN BE found in the roots of most cultures. Some may say that the DNA helix of the human body is itself a mandala. So we find mandalas everywhere since they are the core of our very being. They have representation in all living things. What is inside us surrounds us. It is through and by our human composition that we are bound to the mandala.

The mandala is universal. It does not belong to either the east or the west. We can find it in our own center. We can locate mandalas in a wide variety of cultures; there may be some external differences, but in the center they are the same. They all unite.

Tibetan Buddhism is most commonly associated with the mandala, although mandalas are strong in other Buddhist traditions. The Tibetan mandala depicts a landscape of the Buddhaland or an enlightened vision of a Buddha. Many times the mandala tells a story of the Buddha and other deities and celestial beings. There may be additional mandalas contained within the original one. The mandala is commonly used as a meditation aid and for monks to attain siddhis or supernatural forces. By focusing on images of the divine, one begins to see the divinity within oneself. After several days or weeks of creating the intricate patterns and designs, the mandala is destroyed as a teaching of life's impermanence.

Many Hindu mandalas represent the relationship of the earth, the planets, and the constellations, as well as the elements. The sacred union of opposites is a common theme—the intertwining of two triangles, masculine and feminine, fire and water, Shiva and Shakti—representing the cosmic dance of union and the necessity of this union for the creation and life.

Native Americans have always created mandalas. The medicine wheel is a fine example. It reminds us to honor the spirits of the different directions and the sacred energy in all forms. All creations are brothers and sisters. The legend says that to the north on the medicine wheel is found wisdom. The color for wisdom is white and the medicine animal is the buffalo. The south is represented by the mouse, the color is green. The south is a place for innocence, trust, and for perceiving closely things of nature and of the heart. The west is the bear. The color is black, representing a point of the introspective nature of mankind. The east is marked by the eagle; this is a point of illumination where all things are seen far and wide. Also, very clearly the east is the color of gold or yellow for the morning star. We are each given a particular point at birth on the great wheel; this guides our life. But we must strive to gain knowledge and wisdom from all points to become a whole person.

The Aztec calendar was both a timekeeping device and a religious expression. The Aztec Sunstone calendar looks very similar to some Tibetan sand mandalas.

Muslim and Christian cathedrals contain intricate, ornate, and beautiful stained-glass mandalas. The labyrinths in early Christian churches are mandalas you walk through. The Gothic 12th through 15th century European cathedrals, such as Notre Dame in Paris, were known for their beautiful and ornate rose stained-glass windows. The cathedrals were built during a dark period of plague and war. The sun's illumination symbolized that one must always know that light will exist, even in the most troubling period. These intricate, decorative displays were mandalas that contained both religious and alchemistic symbols.

Mandalas are richly exemplified in the art and architecture of Islam. The crescent moon of Islam represents the lunar calendar while the star represents Allah or the divine.

The Star of David is the most common symbol of modern Judaism. The tree of life is also depicted in a mandala. The Celtic cross is often used to create a mandala symbolizing the blending of the truth and light of the teachings and life of Jesus with the experience of mystical oneness found in the Celtic tradition.

The Pentagram could be said to be a neopagan mandala that expresses the wisdom of the elements and their relationship to one another. In this way the pentacle is not only a magical tool but a teaching tool as well.

Labyrinths are walking mandalas. They are metaphors for a life's journey. They are said to predate Christianity by over a millennium. A well-known labyrinth comes from ancient Crete; it was the lair to mythological creatures. Turf labyrinths exist today in England, Germany, and Scandinavia, and are believed to be linked with the feminine aspects of pagan deities and fertility rituals. In later years the Christian church adopted the labyrinth, and it was common for Christians to make pilgrimages to visit cathedral cities and walk the labyrinth as part of their spiritual journey.

The symbol of Taoism and Chinese dualistic philosophy is a circle divided into two embryonic shapes, one black and the other white. Out of the chaos in the universe came Yang, it represents everything about the world that is illuminated, evident, active, aggressive, controlling, hot, hard, and masculine. Yin, the opposite, represents everything about the world that is dark, hidden, passive, receptive, yielding, cool, soft, and feminine. As opposites, they complemented each other in the formation of a creative force whose products were heaven and earth. The I-Ching coins are also mandalas and they are used as a method of divination of the future.

You could look at all spiritual and religious traditions and find mandalas at their core.

Mandalas Found in Nature

NATURE IS PERHAPS THE ultimate mandala. Nature's symbolism is extremely simple yet at the same time profoundly intricate. Examining the vast interconnectedness of all living things, we can access important insights.

All cultures and human beings are part of nature. In nature, mandalas can be seen wherever we choose to look—the sun, the moon, a multi-petaled daisy, even a shell along the beach. Each object of focus becomes a symbol, a way to open up the mind to a greater understanding of life. By the study of nature we can perceive ourselves as one small particle in the cycle of life and, at the same time, see ourselves as an important component of the whole as well. The sense of separation that is the cause of many of our own and humanity's problems is dissolved as we understand our own contribution to nature.

The mandala of nature is refreshingly uncomplicated. Nature is not subject to divisions of culture. It transcends all boundaries. From nature, we can learn a great deal about how to flow with the tides in our lives. Anyone who tunes in to nature understands that all things are part of the flow of the universe, and each and every part of nature is interdependent upon one another. Because everything that exists naturally is an expression of the sacred, we recognize an infinite power within all.

We need not seclude ourselves from the rest of the world to observe nature as a mandala. You can watch the patterns a flock of birds make as they fly in the sky, or you can sit by a river or lake or even the sea and contemplate the flow of the water. At night you only need to view the sky to see how the stars can communicate. Even in the city, the bright colors of the flowers in a garden can lighten your spirit.

We can also learn so much about ourselves from animals. Although many people see the human being as possessing a higher consciousness, one only needs to observe the family's animal companion to question the idea of superiority. Animals know how to flow with nature on an instinctual basis. They respect the sense of time and wake with the sunrise and sleep at sunset. An animal knows how to live for the moment, something that sages constantly remind us to do in order to experience the happiness of life. Our fellow creatures give all their attention to the needs of each moment, whether it is about eating, playing, or sleeping. They are free from our human anxieties about the past and about the future. By observing animals, we see them as a mandala in motion. By viewing them you can discover more about the various aspects of yourself, leading to an increased sense of wholeness. Through the mandala of nature we see ourselves as part of the whole. We become aware of the simple progression of birth, death, and regeneration that is present in all forms of life.

Mandalas
in Everyday Life

WE SEE THE IMAGE of the mandala everywhere in our daily life. The symbol of the circle can be seen in the construction of our cities, in our homes, and in the accessories we wear. The mandala represents the flow of life. Even some common sayings in our language like "It's come around full circle" and "At the core of the issue" are mandala-inspired words.

Round and geometric shapes have always been an inspiration in home décor. Mandalas are commonly used in the eastern traditions of Vastu and Feng Shui. These philosophies explore the placement and arrangement of furniture in the home or in a place of business to increase positive energy. These traditions use the elements of nature and energy to promote harmonious living in areas of wealth, health, relationships, and all around abundance. They are said to be sciences of directions that combine the five elements of nature and balance them with man and his material surroundings.

More than just architecture or decorating techniques, these traditions help the energy flow in our surroundings. It is the same with the mandalas we create. Through their imagery we can see where we are blocked, and take action to again let our feelings, thoughts, and emotions flow. So the traditions of Vastu and Feng Shui could be said to be mandalas of our homes.

There is a Hindu myth that relates to Vastu. At one point, something formless blocked the sky and the earth. The energy could not move and it created ill thoughts, despair, and disease. Lord Brahma, who is the deity of creation and all things new, knew he needed to do something fast since events were becoming more and more discouraging. He stepped in and decided to take this formless blockage and create it into a spirit; now the formless had a form. He then sat on the spirit's navel or center point, the pivot point of this energy. Brahma instructed other deities to sit on the outer edges of the spirit as well to hold it down. Brahma gave the spirit a name, Vastu Purusha, meaning "the manifested energy." It is a metaphorical expression of the plan of the universe and shows the link between people, buildings, and nature. Brahma said that Vastu Purusha must be pleased before anything new begins. It is viewed as a mandala, a way to balance life, which represents the energy within a building. So now in following the principles of Vastu, all new construction must be "grounded" before work begins. This is usually done by a spiritual ceremony.

Many of the well-loved Islamic mosaics also form mandalas. Each design on the tiles has geometric patterns that create mandalas. A common design is the mandala rosette, which is a pattern based on an eight-pointed star. Spokes emanate from a center point. The eight spokes can be expressed further into 24 or 48 points out or even further still.

In modern décor, we often see the placement of pieces of furniture in a circular or geometric shape to face each other, thus facilitating more convenient conversation. Many business meetings are conducted in a circle so that each individual can be equally heard. In conference rooms where meetings are held, the focal point is a table surrounded by chairs so all seated can face each other. But even our items of decoration are often shaped as a mandala, for instance the rounded shapes of clocks. Perhaps it is further evidence of the continuation of time. Mirrors hung on the wall are also commonly circular. The mirror represents our image of ourselves. What we want to see in our reflection is the perfect mandala—a whole, complete individual who is in unison with his or her surroundings.

A current trend in jewelry is the circle. In a pendant this popular shape is sometimes called the circle-of-life pendant. It is a circular frame with an empty middle. Frequently seen made from bright white diamonds, due to demand it is now designed in sapphires and other gemstones. Jewelers say that next to the heart motif the circle is the most common shape that people request. It represents the continuous nature of life and love. A ring most often means a commitment. A ring is given when one decides to marry another. A popular wedding band is the eternity band. This ring has continuous gemstones around it so you cannot see where it begins or where it ends.

As children we have all played with the enchanting kaleidoscope. Through a series of small mirrors and beads, unique colorful mandalas are formed. Created in 1816 by Scottish scientist Sir David Brewster, kaleidoscopes are still being enjoyed today. He named his invention after the Greek words *kalos* or beautiful, *eidos* or form, and *scopos* or watcher. So kaleidoscope means "the beautiful form watcher." Mirrors are placed in different arrangements to reflect the beads of gems to create varied looks. There are a finite number of mirrors and beads, yet each time a new pattern emerges. Besides creating beauty, kaleidoscopes represent the beauty in change. Although we as individuals evolve and our environment is ever-changing, the relationship between the two stays constant.

Geometric Symbols and Shapes

GEOMETRY IS ONE OF THE oldest sciences. It's the part of mathematics concerned with size, shape, and the position of a figure in relation to time and space. It is the study of shapes and configurations and how they are connected to one another. Geometry corresponds to other theories and sciences including physics, algebra, and astronomy, as well as religion, philosophy, and spirituality. Some call it Sacred Geometry. It assists in answering the question of how materials and things relate to one another. In mandalas, which are a symbol of wholeness, we use the relationship of geometric shapes as an expression of art and how all of existence is related.

Circle

The circle represents the continuum of life. This is why it is one of the most commonly used and seen symbols. The circle can be found everywhere in nature, from the sun up above to the flowers growing in the earth. It is the cycle of life, death, and rebirth. It is karma, action leading to reaction leading to action. The circle is the whole, it represents everything and it also represents nothing. There is no end and no beginning. It is a representation of being present in the now. It is this current moment. It is Universal consciousness, God, creation, and unity.

Square

The square represents seeing from all sides. It stands for mother earth and the four directions: north, south, east, and west. It is to see all from a true perspective, from the same angle, with equal sides and equal angles. It is the representation of the fair judge who, after hearing a legal case, makes a decision not from pre-conceived prejudices or ideas, but from the facts given. It is a central meeting place where everyone is on equal terms. It is a representation of grounded balance.

Triangle

A triangle is a relationship. Each angle is interrelated to the other. It represents the trinity of nature. Body, mind, spirit.

Father, mother, child. Birth, death, resurrection. Father, son, holy spirit. Brahma, Shiva, Vishnu. The three qualities of nature known as the gunas or passion, purity, inertia. It is creation. From two—male and female energy, Shiva and Shakti—a third comes. The triangle is a power symbol; pointing upward it represents grace from heaven above— pyramid power.

Pentagram

The pentagram is known to have magical qualities. It represents the five elements of earth, fire, air, water, and ether. It is also associated with the goddess Venus and its representation of Venus as the morning star, the bringer of light and knowledge. To early Christians the pentagram represented the five wounds of Christ. The Pythagoreans saw the pentagram as mathematical perfection. It has five points, and 5 is a prime number, the sum of 1 and 4, and 2 and 3.

Hexagram

The hexagram is a mandala symbol found in south India's Hindu temples built thousands of years ago. The hexagram symbolizes the state of moksha or a perfect state of balance achieved between man and god, which if maintained would result in liberation of earthly or material trappings.

The hexagram is also thought to be a visual representation of the Hebrew name David. Its shape is two of the three letters in the biblical Hebrew spelling of the name. The symbol may have been a simple family crest formed by flipping and juxtaposing the two most prominent letters in the name. Some researchers have theorized that the hexagram represents the astrological chart at the time of David's birth. The hexagram is also known as the "King's Star" in astrological circles.

Other Shapes

Other symbols used in mandalas include the indestructible diamond, a symbol of the nature of the mind. It is clear, but when viewed, all colors can be seen. The bell represents the female in tantric polarity. It is boundless and open to receiving wisdom. The vajra represents the male in tantric polarity. It is a sign of Buddha's active compassion with the meditating person. The dharma wheel has eight spindles or hubs that show the eightfold path to enlightenment. The paths are right belief, right resolution, right speech, right action, right living, right effort, right thinking, and peace of mind through meditation. Lastly, the lotus is a symbol of the teaching of the Buddha. The lotus, a breathtaking flower, has its roots in the mud and yet grows through the mud and the water raising its blossom towards the light. The lotus is a representation of how we should live daily.

Commonly Used Colors in Mandalas

COLOR IS ALL around us. It affects us today as it did thousands of years ago when people's daily existence was ruled by the light of the day and the darkness of the night. Most living things are influenced by color. They become vitalized and empowered by the bright reds, oranges, and yellows of daylight, and calmed and relaxed by the blues, indigos, and purples of the night. Color is an important part of symbolism and culture. Color is a language of its own. It speaks about emotions and feelings as well as relaying a physical force. Color can be used to influence our well-being; different hues will either stimulate our mind or relax it. Following is a list of some of the common meanings for the various colors you can use when creating your mandala art.

Red

Red is heat, passion, fire. It is associated with energy and is all-consuming. It is identified with the life force since it is the color of blood. It is enthusiasm and ambition. It is also associated with victory. Red is extremely visible. It wants to be noticed. Red is the color of romantic love and considered good luck in many cultures. In the east, brides wear red for success in their marriage.

Blue

Blue is a serene, cool color. It is associated with the calm of the sea and the vastness of the sky. It is depth, wisdom, and loyalty. Blue is also the color for communication and knowledge. It is considered beneficial to both the mind and the body. Blue is said to promote tranquility and calmness. It also alleviates worries and distress. Many religions consider blue to be the color of God since it represents truth.

Green

Green is the color of nature. It is seen everywhere in the trees, in the grass, in the stems of flowers. It represents growth, abundance, harmony, and freshness. Green is a color that can help bring balance to the body and help cleanse the mind. It is related to the heart, which is in the center and hence is associated with love and rejections. Green helps to suck the negativity from a person and emit only positive energy. The color green also has healing properties for digestion. When one sees the lush green fields, a sense of joy seeps through the body. This effect on a human being is only provided by this color. Emotionally we associate green with safety, and it is known to have healing powers for those who view it.

Yellow

Yellow is brightness, happiness, and joy. It is the color of sunshine. It is the color of light. It brings cheerful, pleasant feelings. Yellow also helps in removing the energy blocks at the core level and has a healing influence on the human body and mind. Because it is an associate to gold, it is considered a regal and sacred color.

Orange

Orange is a warm, tropical color. It is a color of fascination, attraction, encouragement, and success. Orange increases the blood supply to the brain and stimulates appetite. This color is also the king of creativity and imagination. Because it helps in the stimulation of the brain, it gives vent to a person's creative juices. Though orange is more ambitious and self-sufficient, it lacks the warmth of red. It is used in psychological medicine to bring joy and cure grief. This color is so bright that it overcomes the dark gloominess and helps in protecting oneself when the need arises. It is also a color of spirituality and was the color the Buddha chose to wear.

Pink

Pink is associated with an open heart. It has a soft, compassionate, feminine vibe. It is an approachable color. It is a soothing tone on a physical, mental, and emotional level. It can be used to dissipate feelings of anger and neglect. Pink can also be used to awaken love and purity. It is a spiritual color that helps to bring focus if meditating on it.

Purple

Purple is the color of wisdom and it is known to calm the mind and the nerves. It is the color that has medicinal and healing properties. It helps in calming a person and is used to lessen pain in all organs, relax the muscles, and calm the nervous system. It is also associated with the inner consciousness. Purple is a dream color; it helps a person's dream activity. It is the combination of blue and red, hence it has the properties of both these colors as well as the planets Mars and Saturn. Mars is an earthy planet whereas Saturn is spiritual. Hence violet has the balance of both the physical and spiritual aspects. It evokes a majestic feeling and is associated with wealth, mystery, and magic. Purple is balance and its uplifting qualities encourage creativity in all.

Indigo

Think of the midnight sky and think of indigo. It is a mystical color of wisdom. Associated with spiritual and self-realization, it is the outward communication of blue turned inward. It is reflection, profound insight, and instant understanding. It is the color of all-knowing and psychic intuition. Indigo is the color of invention.

Brown

Brown says reliability, stability, approachability. It is thought of as neutral and is the color of our earth. It brings about feelings of wholesomeness and orderliness. It is a balancing color. Though not a primary color, it helps in maintaining the balance of the body, mind, and soul. This color is a mixture of the primary colors black and red. Saturn is the planet associated with this color and Capricorn is the zodiac sign for it. Since mother earth is brown in color, it brings stability. People who like this color are practical, simple, and very down-to-earth. This color helps in financial emergencies. It also helps in decision making and concentration. Brown gives warmth to certain people yet for some it can be depressing. People who do not like brown don't like the routine and sameness in life. People who like this color are family-oriented and have loyal friends. It's a natural color that evokes a sense of strength and reliability to the wearer. It is an effective color in healing. Brown calms highly strung and emotional people and relaxes their mental state.

White

White is light, innocence, and purity. It is considered a color of perfection. It possesses a high vibration of spiritual energy.

This color is associated with the moon. Just like the moon is cool and serene, this color is also beautiful and gives dignity. The gemstone is pearl and the elegance of pearl is known to one and all. The color white is often associated with uprightness, wisdom, and honesty. In weddings, the bride wears white to signify her innocence and femininity. White is also the color for domestic happiness. This color is generally favorable to most of the zodiac signs. Wearing white for official purpose gives good luck. Many religious leaders and clergy choose to wear white as a symbol of modesty. White is also the color of resurrection of the spirit and is commonly used in celebrations of new beginnings as well as in the mourning of death.

Black

Black is the color of neutrality. It signifies power and formality as well as death and mystery. It gives a feeling of depth and perspective as well as the fear of unknown. This color is like a shadow to the other colors and does not have any planet associated with it. Some don't consider black a color at all, rather they view it as the lack of color. According to Indian mythology the black shadow is of Saturn, who is the illegitimate son of the sun god, looks dark, and is handicapped. Black is also associated with blindness and emotions like temper, tantrums, and negative feelings. But black can alleviate the negative energy let out by other people. Since Saturn is the ruler of Capricorn, black color brings luck to these people. It is the remover of all obstacles and hindrances in a person's life. It wards off evil and keeps away the negative energy. The gemstone black onyx gives very good results when teamed with diamonds or pearls, and also looks attractive on the wearer. It shows the person is determined and steadfast in his approach to the job he sets out to finish. Black is necessary since it brings balance to whatever hue it is next to. Black is also associated with spirituality.

Gray

The color gray is known to be neutral. It is a tone of balance since it is the merging of black and white. Gray is conservative and represents security, maturity, and dependability. As a responsible color, its energy imparts void, emptiness, and detachment. It is a cool color in all senses of the word. Although it is not usually a favorite color, it is commonly seen in dress and environments due to its stabilizing effect on the psyche. It is said that gray assists in bringing commitment to relationships.

The Psychological Benefits of Mandalas

FOR THOUSANDS OF years, as well as today, different cultures used the symbol of the mandala for healing. Native Americans used the mandala, the medicine wheel, to tend to the sick and guide the future. Buddhist monks used the mandala not only to connect to the divine, but also for individual and global healing. In our western culture, mandalas are now being used as therapy. They help to treat the emotional problems that may or may not be connected to a physical aliment. Perhaps the forerunner to using mandalas as therapy in western society is Carl Jung.

Carl Jung was a theoretical and practicing clinical psychologist. He had a broad and unique approach to psychology that included viewing metaphysics, dreams, archetypes, etc., when treating his patients. He spent much of his life exploring eastern and western philosophy, alchemy, astrology, and sociology as well as literature and the arts. He is known for his concept of psychological archetype, the collective unconscious, and his theory of synchronicity.

Jung knew and emphasized the importance of balance and harmony in one's life. He felt that humankind would benefit from integrating spirituality into science and logic. Jung traveled worldwide and, when in India, became fascinated with eastern philosophies and religions, incorporating them into his key concepts of ideology, including the idea of incorporating spirituality into everyday life and appreciation of the unconscious.

He developed his own specialized style and approach to the study of the human mind. For Jung to understand the soul he delved into the world of dreams and myths. He explored the human experience with the unconscious through symbols and archetypal forces.

Jung felt that the collective unconscious is composed of archetypes or familiar symbols. He theorized that certain symbolic themes exist across all cultures, all epochs, and in every individual. For Jung, the mandala was a symbol of wholeness, completeness, and perfection. The mandala did not only mirror an inner state of order for him, he felt its harmony or disharmony also encompasses the environment of the individual.

Mandalas were defined by Jung as magic circles that contained certain design motifs he found to have a universal nature, across cultures and across time. It did not matter whether they were the transiently created mandalas from Tibet, sand paintings from the American southwest, or illustrations from ancient, medieval, and Renaissance alchemical works.

Jung believed mandalas were a map that explained the state of the self as it was on the day the mandala was created. He also believed that mandalas appeared in connection with dreams, chaotic psychic states of disorientation or panic, and that a function of the mandalas is to bring order out of chaos. Through his own mandala practice, Jung was eventually led to understand mandalas as symbols of the self—they are informed by archetypal forces in the unconscious that the artist is not aware of during the creation of the work.

He thought the mandala symbolically represents that path to the center. Jung's later practice included having his patients spontaneously create mandalas; it's a prime example of Jung's own explorations into the unconscious becoming effective tools in his psychiatric practice. He found there was a universality of the symbolism used by his patients. Jung's reasoning for the similarity in mandala symbols created by his patients is that these symbols and images come from the collective uncon-scious and are therefore archetypes, or primordial images, that reside in each of us.

"I had to abandon the idea of the super ordinate position of the ego. I saw that everything, all paths I had been fol-lowing, all steps I had taken, were leading back to a single point, namely, to the midpoint. It became increasingly plain to me that the mandala is the centre. It is the exponent of all path. It is the path to the centre, to individuation. . . . I knew that in finding the mandala as an expression of the self I had attained what was for me the ultimate." C.G. Jung from *Memories, Dreams, Reflections*

Jung was the first to use mandalas in therapy when he found that the act of drawing mandalas had a calming and healing effect on patients. The mandala serves as a symbolic representation of emotionally contained feelings, and yet at the same time provides a sense of order and integration to the feelings. Drawing a mandala serves a similar function to written or spoken disclosure in that it provides organization to complex emotional experiences.

Today many art therapists use the mandala as a basic tool for self-awareness, self-expression, conflict resolution, and healing. Within the realm of art therapy, the mandala generally refers to any art form that is executed within a circular context. The mandala has been found to be an effective therapeutic tool within numerous populations and settings including schizophrenia and psychotic disorders; Attention-Deficit Hyperactivity Disorder; cancer survivors; physically and emotionally abused individuals; and individuals with high levels of anxiety and panic attacks. In truth, mandala art as therapy can be used for everyone at any time. It is a way of expressing what we are thinking, feeling, and experiencing.

Mandalas can be thought of as conscious dreaming. You can be your own therapist if you like, meaning that you do not need a degree to express yourself through your mandala art. The colors, patterns, and shapes you use can be an indication of the positive and negative emotions you are feeling. There is no right or wrong to a mandala you create.

Mandalas as Power Tools of the Mind

MANDALAS ARE A powerful tool for meditation because the mind creates its strongest associations through imagery. The majority of the people in the world are visual in nature. They need to see something to relate to it. If you say or think of a flower, a person, or an event, an image will immediately arise in your mind. A mandala is intensely visual, energized with color and enlivened with design. Once pictured and absorbed into the mind, changes in your mental state occur to influence your emotions. Your perception is enhanced and a heightened state of awareness and insights can surface. What you feel is directly related to your state of being. The creation of a mandala helps to bring out the complexity of what is happening inside. The meditation enables you to perceive more clearly and helps how you approach the ups and downs of daily life.

When we visibly focus on one point, the mind becomes infatuated with that point. At first the mind will wander, go from one thought to another, moving away from the original theme. As you bring the mind back to the focus, the mind understands and trains itself to retain its focus. At that point the mind looks forward to the focus and the concentration is set. The infatuation has begun. The majority of people have problems letting go. It is a challenge for most individuals to go with the flow. The average person dwells in the past and frets about the future. Think about it. When was the last time that your concentration was on the present? When was the last time you were in the here and now? Using a mandala assists in staying in the now. The mandala serves as pure beauty, something you can not stay away from. When your focus is set, either in the preparation and creation of your mandala or of your meditation on the completed design, you can now allow the powerful inspiration of the mandala to be released.

The aim of meditation is to quiet the mind. Within the stillness that arises from this is found a sense of deep tranquility and harmony. The nature of the mind is to move, to think, to interact, and to be busy. Thoughts constantly come and go, hopping from one subject to another. It is hard to concentrate with all of this happening. This is true whether you are working on and creating your mandala or viewing it. Part of the practice is keeping your attention steady.

The act of meditation is extremely simple and at the same time the hardest challenge. Many who learn the techniques of meditation will ask something like, "Is that all there is?" The principles of meditation are easy to learn but hard to maintain in practice because the mind is stubborn and set in its ways. Meditation is a commitment; it is not learned and mastered in just a few days. With regular dedication and patient practice, progress will come. Take the time for meditation as you would take the time for a special appointment. It is helpful to schedule it at a specific time each day, just like a business meeting. It is said that one needs to take care of oneself first before taking care of anyone else. In order for us to be productive in life we need to nurture ourselves so we can be grounded, focused, and refreshed. Realize that your meditation may be the most important thing you do all day. So before you begin, turn off the television and definitely shut off your phone. Give yourself the attention you deserve.

Meditation Practices

The following exercises will help you clear your mind, center yourself, and collect your energy by focusing on mandalas or natural elements. Concentration is everything at first, but it is the concentration of letting go.

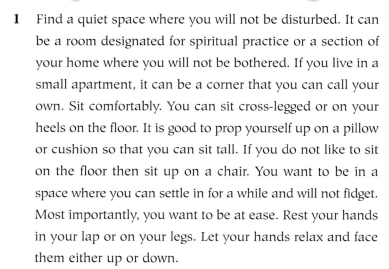

Seated Mandala Meditation

1   Find a quiet space where you will not be disturbed. It can be a room designated for spiritual practice or a section of your home where you will not be bothered. If you live in a small apartment, it can be a corner that you can call your own. Sit comfortably. You can sit cross-legged or on your heels on the floor. It is good to prop yourself up on a pillow or cushion so that you can sit tall. If you do not like to sit on the floor then sit up on a chair. You want to be in a space where you can settle in for a while and will not fidget. Most importantly, you want to be at ease. Rest your hands in your lap or on your legs. Let your hands relax and face them either up or down.

2   Place your chosen mandala at eye level and at least an arm's length away from you. If you would like, the mandala can be further away, depending on its size. You want to be able to see the whole mandala as well as its various parts.

3   Bring your gaze to the mandala but look softly. Do not stare or be tense. Your eyes should be relaxed. To begin, take in the whole image, allowing the eyes to rest on one point. If your eyes dart a bit or you see a double image, don't worry. Blink only as necessary. Remain focused on the image. If your attention wanders, bring it back each time to the mandala. Try not to think about the mandala,

or to access the meaning or critique the design. Simply look at it, steadily and evenly.

At the beginning, practice for five minutes each day. Stay within a time limit in which you feel comfortable. Practicing with a kitchen timer is helpful when you are starting—not worrying about time will be one less distraction. As you become used to this form of meditation, you can extend the minutes that you sit. A session lasting 20 or 30 minutes is a good practice, but work within your own schedule. Never push yourself to sit longer or stress yourself out. Mandala meditation is a joyous experience, not a chore. You can change the mandala you are viewing whenever you feel it is right. It is a good idea to spend several or more sessions with one pattern and not be so quick to look at another. In mandala meditation practice, you approach the image without conscious preconceptions and let it take you where it will.

Visual Mandala Meditation

1   Find a quiet space where you will not be disturbed. It can be a room designated for spiritual practice, or a section of your home where you will not be bothered. If you live in a small apartment, it can be a corner that you can call your own. Sit comfortably. You can sit cross-legged or on your heels on the floor. It is good to prop yourself up on a pillow

or cushion so that you can sit tall. If you do not like to sit on the floor then sit up on a chair. You want to be in a space where you can settle in for a while and will not fidget. Most importantly, you want to be at ease. Rest your hands in your lap or on your legs. Let your hands relax and face them either up or down.

2   Place your chosen mandala at eye level and at least an arm's length away from you. If you would like, the mandala can be further away, depending on its size. You want to be able to see the whole mandala as well as its various parts.

3   Bring your gaze to the mandala and focus your complete attention on it. Stare at it for at least a minute or two. Now close your eyes and try to recreate the image in your mind's eye. See if you can visualize the mandala without looking at it. When you lose the visualization, open your eyes again, look at the picture, and repeat.

You can practice Visual Mandala Meditation for 5 minutes or up to 20 or more minutes per day. If you get stressed or anxious during the day, you can always visualize your mandala to regain your peace. The effect of this meditation practice is to reground yourself whenever you need to.

Creative Mandala Meditation

1   Find a quiet space where you will not be disturbed. It can be a room designated for spiritual practice, or a section of your home where you will not be bothered. If you live in a small apartment, it can be a corner that you can call your own. Sit comfortably. You can sit cross-legged or on your heels on the floor. It is good to prop yourself up on a pillow or cushion so that you can sit tall. If you do not like to sit on the floor then sit up on a chair. If you would like, you can even lay on the floor for this practice. You want to be in a space where you can settle in for a while. Most importantly, you want to be at ease. Have a paper and pencil or pen ready to jot down your inspirations.

2   Place your chosen mandala in front of you so you can view the entire image.

3   Bring your gaze to the mandala but with softly focused eyes. Look at the image and let your thoughts wander around the subject of the mandala. Whatever the thoughts are, whether they are on the pattern, the color, or the symbolism, let the thoughts come.

4   If you choose, write down your feelings and inspirations as they flow. Do not feel pressured. Some sessions will not produce light-bulb ideas. Put on paper anything that you feel could be significant, even if it's only a word or two.

It is a nice idea to work with one mandala image for a few days or weeks. You can even go back to a mandala after leaving it alone for several months. Save the comments that you made and compare them from previous sessions. Observe your trends of thoughts and insights and see how they can apply to your life.

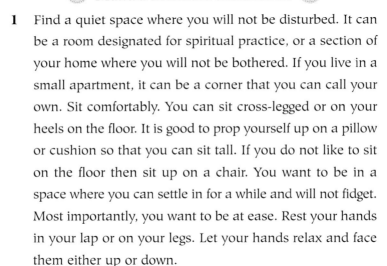 *Mantra Mandala Meditation*

1   Find a quiet space where you will not be disturbed. It can be a room designated for spiritual practice, or a section of your home where you will not be bothered. If you live in a small apartment, it can be a corner that you can call your own. Sit comfortably. You can sit cross-legged or on your heels on the floor. It is good to prop yourself up on a pillow or cushion so that you can sit tall. If you do not like to sit on the floor then sit up on a chair. You want to be in a space where you can settle in for a while and will not fidget. Most importantly, you want to be at ease. Rest your hands in your lap or on your legs. Let your hands relax and face them either up or down.

2   Place your chosen mandala at eye level and at least an arm's length away from you. If you would like, the mandala can be further away, depending on its size. You want to be able to see the whole mandala as well as its various parts.

3   Bring your gaze to the mandala but softly. Choose a mantra that you would like to repeat. You may find it helpful to

choose one that corresponds to your mandala theme. A nice Buddhist mantra is Om Mani Padma Hum. Although it is said there is no direct translation, it could be said to mean, "Behold, the jewel is in the Lotus." This mantra is said to encompass all the teachings of the Buddha.

Other suggested mantras include:
God is love.
Wisdom is within.
Sat-yam: I am truth.
I am an important part of nature and the universe.
Om Namah Shivah: a yogi's chant to be open to change.
The Lord is my shepherd, I shall not want.
Divine wisdom flows through me.

Nature Meditation—Meditation on the Moon

This meditation can be done every day from the half moon all the way up to the full moon. The moon represents our intuitive side, which helps to develop insight and those "aha" moments.

1   Find a peaceful place. In the spring, summer, and fall months you may want to sit outside to get a clear, full view of the moon. In the winter, you can stay inside and look at the moon from a window.

2   Begin to gaze at the moon and see if you can view as many details as possible. Perhaps observe the color or

the shading of the moon's surface. See if you spot ridges or craters. You can even observe the clouds nearby.

3   Use this time to observe the moon so deeply that there is only you and the moon.

4   Feel the connection and know you are part of the universe.

5   You can practice from 5 minutes to 30 minutes.

Nature Meditation—Meditation on a Flower

1   Find a quiet space where you will not be disturbed. It can be a room designated for spiritual practice, or a section of your home where you will not be bothered. If you live in a small apartment, it can be a corner that you can call your own. In the warmer months, you may want to sit outside in a garden. Sit comfortably. You can sit cross-legged or on your heels on the floor or ground. It is good to prop yourself up on a pillow or cushion so that you can sit tall. If you do not like to sit on the floor or ground then sit up on a chair. You want to be in a space where you can settle in for a while.

2   Either hold your favorite flower or a picture of one. Begin to focus on your breath. Focus on the inhale and focus on the exhale.

3   Bring your attention to the flower. Allow your gaze to be soft—not staring or hard. Do not strain your eyes. Keep your attention on the flower. Notice its color. Notice the petals.

Notice its core. When you view the details of the flower, try not to analyze them. Just observe. Simply be conscious of the beauty of the flower. Now reverse. Notice the core of the flower and move outward towards the flower. Know there is no distinction between you and the flower. The flower is inside of you. You possess the same beauty.

4   Sit with your flower for several minutes. Then let the flower rest. Let your eyes close. Go back to your breath focus. This meditation will give you an understanding and appreciation of all of the natural beauty in the world.

Walking Mandala Meditation

1   Depending on where you live, you may need to be creative with the mandala space in your mind. You can practice this meditation in a park or in the city. Begin by looking at a map. If no map is available you can draw one yourself. You want to create a round area for your map. What you are doing is creating your own labyrinth. A labyrinth can be thought of as a walking mandala.

2   Once you have your map, figure out where the center is. If you are in a park you can designate a tree, a statute, or even a park bench as the center. If in a city you can decide on a building or a street corner as your hub or center. From there you want to figure out the outer edge of your circle, which is where you will start. Many people feel that they

need to have a maze in order to create a labyrinth. Even if you can see your center clearly with no blocks of vision, you can still enjoy this meditation.

3   Now begin to walk. Do not preplan how to get to your center, but allow yourself to be taken by the moment. A labyrinth is about trusting in the path and allowing yourself to let go. It is a testament to the old saying of "let go and let God."

4   As you continue on your walk pay close attention to your surroundings. Try not to think about what you did before you started your journey, or about what you need to do later. Do not bother with the time. Allow yourself to be present.

5   As best as you can, depending on the environment, try to walk in a circular movement. In other words, fill out your area and do not rush to find your center.

6   When you finally reach your central point, you may want to sit for a few minutes and jot down or evaluate what you discovered. You may have noticed your surroundings in a whole new way. You may have seen a tree for the first time. You may have noticed a nuance of a building. A labyrinth is an exercise in creativity and intuition. It helps to connect our inner world with our outer world.

Channeling Energy Through Mandalas

AS MENTIONED EARLIER, THE aim of meditation is to quiet the mind. Within the stillness that arises from this is found a sense of deep tranquility and harmony. The nature of the mind is to move, to think, to interact, and to be busy. Thoughts constantly come and go, hopping from one subject to another. With all of this happening it is hard to concentrate, even if you are working on and creating your mandala or simply viewing it.

A yantra is a form of a mandala used for concentration. It is a geometric representation of levels and energies of the cosmos that also correlates with the human body. Yantras are commonly used in the tantric yogic path where the yantra is treated as a symbol of one's chosen deity or god. Yantras can be drawn on paper, wood, cloth, or inscribed on metal and other materials. They usually consist of a square, circles, lotus petals, triangles, and a central point known as the bindu point. This point represents the gateway to enlightenment. The practitioner visualizes and internalizes the yantra until he or she becomes one with the image. The most commonly known yantras are contained within the chakra system.

The Chakra System

The word *chakra* means wheel or vortex; chakras are major psychic centers in the subtle body responsible for specific physiological and psychic functions. They are associated with mandalas due to their circular shape and because through concentration and the drawing of their symbol or image they can promote a change in either a psychic, emotional, or metaphysical way. They are not tangible although they do link to parts and systems of the human body. There are seven major chakras and there is some debate on how many minor ones—some say two and some say at least 21. There are six different symbols that the images of a chakra have in common: the chakra color, the petal of the lotus flower, the yantra or geometrical shape, a bija (or seed) mantra, an animal, and a deity or divine being.

The lotus symbolizes man's growth from the lowest states of awareness to the higher states of consciousness. In the same way that the culmination of the growth of the lotus is a beautiful flower, so is the culmination of man's spiritual quest in the awakening and blossoming of human potential. The animal represents man's previous evolution and instincts, and the divine being represents higher consciousness. The chakras are archetypes of right action and living. People are always talking about opening up the chakras and each person has their own set of circumstances on which they need to work. In opening the chakras our consciousness and mind undergo changes. These changes have a significant relevance and relationship with everyday life.

The first chakra is known as the mooladhara chakra. The Sanskrit word *moola* means root or foundation and that is what this chakra is. It influences the root of our whole existence. The impulses of life rise through the body and flower as we expand our awareness. It seems a great paradox that this earthiest and most basic chakra guides to the highest level. The mooladhara chakra is located in the male body slightly inside the perineum, midway between the scrotum and the anus. In the female body, the mooladhara chakra lies on the posterior side of the cervix.

The mooladhara chakra is traditionally represented by a lotus flower with four deep crimson petals. A golden yellow square is a yantra representing the earth element, supported by an elephant with seven trunks. The elephant is the largest of all land animals and possesses great strength and solidity. He represents the deity Ganesh who has a great mind and creativity. Riding on the elephant's back in the center of the square is a deep red inverted triangle. Within the triangle is a lingam. This represents Shiva/Shakti or creative energy. Focusing on this mandala of moola bhanda, one can become fearless, grounded, and content with life.

Swadhisthana is the name for the second point. The Sanskrit word *swa* means one's own and *adhisthana* means dwelling place or residence. Swadhisthana is located at the base of the spinal column, at the level of the coccyx or tailbone. It is depicted as a six-petaled orange lotus. A white crescent moon within the lotus represents the store of formless karma. A crocodile symbolizes the phantom of unconscious fears in life and how we must become aware that our actions today reflect our results of tomorrow. Vishnu is the deity who reflects on the preservation of wholeness in our daily existence.

The third chakra is manipura. The word is derived from two Sanskrit words: *mani* meaning jewel and *pura* meaning city. Therefore, manipura means "city of jewels." In the Tibetan tradition this chakra is known as mani padma or jeweled lotus. Manipura is very important. It is the center of dynamism, energy, will, and achievement, and is often compared to the dazzling heat and power of the sun. Manipura radiates and distributes pranic energy throughout the entire human framework, regulating and energizing the various activities of organs and systems of life. When deficient, the individual is lifeless, devoid of energy, and will be hindered by poor health, depression, and lack of motivation. So meditating on or coloring this chakra mandala is important for anyone who wants to enjoy life.

The manipura chakra is located directly behind the navel on the inner wall of the spinal column. This chakra is anatomically related to the solar plexus, which controls the digestive fire and heat regulation of the body. The symbol of manipura is a ten-petaled bright yellow lotus. In the center of the lotus is a ring of fire, depicted by an inverted fiery red triangle that shines like the rising sun. A ram shows the dynamism and endurance of this chakra. The deity is an aspect of Shiva, representing the cycle of change. To meditate on this area is to gain knowledge of the entire physical system. When this center is purified and awakened, the body becomes disease-free and luminous.

The fourth chakra, anahata, translates to mean unstruck or unbeated. This center is known as such because of its relationship with the heart, which throbs, beats, or vibrates to a constant unbroken rhythm. It is said in many of the ancient scriptures that there is a sound that is non-physical; it is transcendental in nature. This sound is endless and unbroken in the same way that the heart beats faithfully and continuously from before birth up until death. Anahata is situated in the spinal column on the inner wall, directly behind the center of the chest. It is the heart center but that does not mean our physical heart. It is the space in the heart where purity resides. This chakra is connected to the part of the brain that is responsible for all the creative sciences and fine arts such as painting, dance, music, poetry, etc. The symbol of anahata is blue and has twelve petals. The inner region is a hexagonal shape. It is made up of two interlaced triangles, symbolizing the union of consciousness and creativity. An antelope represents alertness and lightness of foot and being. Isha, an aspect of the deity Vishnu, represents universal love. Tantric scriptures say that in anahata thoughts and desires are fulfilled. The first preparation to opening Anahata is to change your entire way of thinking. You must become extremely optimistic and positive, always full of hope. You also must always be at peace with yourself, physically and mentally, regardless of conflicts in the world.

The fifth chakra, vishuddhi, is known as the purification center. The Sanskrit word *shuddhi* means to purify and in the chakra the purifying and harmonizing of all opposites takes place. It represents a flowing with life, allowing things to happen as they must. Proper understanding and true discrimination come from meditating on this chakra mandala. It is said that the mind becomes pure. Vishuddhi is located behind the throat pit and it is symbolized by a sixteen-petaled purple or green lotus. A snow-white elephant and the deity Sadashiva represent consciousness of the etheric plane. When this area is awakened it is said that the spirit of youth returns.

Ajna chakra is the point of psychic connection. It is where individual consciousness begins to understand super consciousness and realize they are two of the same. The word *ajna* comes from the Sanskrit root word which means to know, to obey, or to follow. Literally ajna means command or the monitoring center. In astrology ajna is the center of Jupiter, which symbolizes the guru or great teacher. It is where one receives revelations and insight on the nature of existence. Ajna chakra, the sixth, is located in the brain directly behind the eyebrow center. It is at the very top of the spinal cord, at the medulla oblongata. The symbol of ajna is a two-petaled white or violet lotus. Shiva is the deity and represents transformation. Studying the ajna chakra is the way towards seeing the divinity within.

The seventh chakra, sahasrara, is known as the crown chakra since it is based and hovers over the top of the head. It represents the coming together of all the other chakras, almost like turning on the light. It illuminates the reason for our existence. The meaning of sahasrara is one thousand. It is for this reason that it is said to be a thousand-petaled lotus. It also implies magnitude, significance, and vastness so sahasrara should really be described as an infinite number of petals. It is everything. Meditating on this chakra mandala helps one to see that there is no I, nor you, nor them, it is only one.

Creating a Mandala

THE MANDALA, besides being used to decorate and sanctify a temple or a home, can be used as an offering. This offering can be made to one's teacher or guru, or to the universe, as a gift or payment for the preciousness of the teachings. Creating a Mandala can be an unselfish act of offering your time, energy, and patience to a higher cause, or it can be a lesson to uncover more about your true nature.

Mandalas can be found in every culture. When you look at the source of their symbolism, it is tied to how man is united and connected with the universe or the divine. In Tibet, all monks living in monasteries are required to learn how to construct mandalas as part of their training. The learning process is twofold. It includes the memorization of texts that specify the names, lengths, and positions of the primary lines that define the basic structure of mandalas. It also includes the manual techniques of how to draw and use various materials. But it is really the repetition of creating a mandala over and over again where the true learning of the craft comes in. The more you practice creating a mandala, the easier it becomes and the more it can be about the intention behind the mandala. It is said that at the Namgyal monastery, the personal monastery of the Dalai Lama, this period of learning is about three years.

Mandalas are commonly made from paper, textiles, sand, shells, flowers, rice, or gemstones. In sand painting, the sand is dyed and then carefully placed on a large, flat table. The construction process takes several days and the mandala is destroyed shortly after its completion.

Monks from the Buddhist tradition make impermanent mandalas using materials such as flowers, crushed stones and gemstones, grains of rice that have been dyed, and colored grains of sand. Sand that is made from crushed precious gemstones is considered to be the most effective since the precious stones are earth's natural treasures. Each grain of sand is charged with the blessings of the ritual process, producing spiritual energy that emits from the mandala. The Tibetan word for mandala is *kilkhor,* which generally means center of the circle with exteriors, walls, and surrounding environment.

Each mandala is believed to be a sacred mansion, housing a particular deity who represents and embodies enlightened qualities ranging from compassion to heightened consciousness and bliss. Both the deity and the mandala itself are recognized as pure expressions of the Buddha's realized or enlightened mind. The more times a monk creates a mandala the purer his intention becomes—the more he connects with the nature of the Buddha.

Traditional Tibetan Mandala Construction

Before a monk can construct a mandala, he must study for years and undergo technical artistic training and memorization. He must know how to draw all of the symbols, deities, and philosophical concepts. When the construction of the mandala is just beginning, the monks sit around the drawn-out mandala base. As the process continues, depending upon the mandala's size, the monks eventually stand.

The mandala is usually divided into four quadrants and one monk is assigned to each. Although the monk works on his portion alone, he knows that when finished it may not be noticeable that several monks worked on the entire project. The monks memorize each detail of the mandala. The design of the mandala is not a conceptual process, rather it is one created from scripture. At the end of each day, the monks dedicate their work to the benefit of others. The reason why the monks put so much effort and care into their work is that they believe they are imparting the Buddha's teachings in the creation of the mandala. Since the visuals of the mandala contain guidelines by the Buddha on attaining enlightenment, the purity of their intention and actions allows the viewer the most benefit.

Each detail in all four areas or quadrants of the mandala faces the center, in order for it to face the deity of the mandala. In the most common form of the mandala, it appears as a series of concentric circles. Each mandala has its own deity in the square structure situated concentrically within these circles. The perfect square shape is a reflection of the absolute space of wisdom. The four sides of the square represent loving kindness, compassion, sympathy, and equanimity. The square is described as a palace since it is the residence of the deity of the mandala, and because it contains the essence of the Buddha.

The series of circles that surrounds the central square has an intense symbolic meaning. In the outer circles, often a ring of fire is depicted, which symbolizes the process of transformation of man. There may also be a thunderbolt or some diamond scepters, known as vajra, indicating the indestructibility and diamond-like brilliance of the mandala's spiritual makeup. Frequently other circles contain representations of human consciousness and how it is tied to the cycle of birth and rebirth.

The deity is in the center of the mandala. It is the power of this deity that gives the essence and force of the mandala. The deity could be peaceful, wrathful, or sexual. The peaceful deity is usually a representation of compassion, wisdom, or courage and strength in the search for sacred knowledge. Wrathful deities may suggest man's struggle in his search for enlightenment. Wrathful deities are representations of man's inner turmoil, which is tamed by spiritual practice. Sexual imagery represents the male and female elements that interconnect for wholeness. It is sometimes used as a metaphor for satisfaction, contentment, unity, and enlightenment.

In creating a mandala, both the artist and the viewer are reminded of the vastness of the universe and its potential within themselves. According to the Buddhist path, the purpose of a mandala is to put an end to human suffering, to attain enlightenment, and to see a correct view of reality. It is to see that divinity resides within oneself.

Constructing a Mandala Using Pencils and Paper—Simple Version

Materials needed:

12" square of paper, a nice-quality heavy paper if possible

A round plate—you may want to have two, one smaller than the other

Different colored pencils or pens

A pencil sharpener

An eraser

Procedures:

Give yourself the time to create your mandala, perhaps an hour or so. You may want to put on your favorite music, but turn off your phone.

Before you begin, you may want to clarify the intention of your design or give a word of thanks to the universe. You also may want to request guidance and insight so it is your inner teacher who is creating your mandala. Use your intuition and allow a shape or color that comes to you to be reflected in your work.

Place your plate on the paper and trace around it with a light-color pencil.

If you choose, you can put a smaller circle within the larger one.

Now fill in the circle with whatever you feel belongs there. Use whatever shapes, colors, and combinations feel right to you. There are no rules with this mandala. All decisions are correct. Also there are no accidents. Even if you draw something that is not in your plan, do not erase it, rather go with it and see where it leads you.

Allow your inner spirit to express itself onto paper.

Once your mandala is finished, put the date you completed it. You may want to note how long it took you—the number of hours or the number of days.

Hang your mandala on a wall or on your refrigerator where you can see it regularly. Each day spend a few minutes simply looking at it, and allow it to explain itself to you. As you get thoughts on its various meanings, write these observations down around your mandala. This is a nice way of remembering what emotions you were feeling or exploring at that time in your life.

Constructing a Mandala Using Pencils and Paper—More Complicated Version

Materials needed:

12" square of paper, a nice-quality heavy paper if possible

A compass

A protractor

A ruler

Different colored pencils or pens

A pencil sharpener

An eraser

Procedures:

Give yourself the time to create your mandala, perhaps an hour or so. You may want to put on your favorite music, but turn off your phone.

Before you begin, you may want to clarify the intention of your design or give a word of thanks to the universe. You also may want to request guidance and insight so it is your inner teacher who is creating your mandala. Use your intuition and allow a shape or color that comes to you to be reflected in your work.

With a compass and a pencil, construct concentric circles on 12" paper. Make sure there is irregular distance between the circles. Draw some very close together, some farther apart. Create anywhere from 12 to 18 concentric circles. Make these circles very light because they will only really serve as guidelines for parts of the upcoming design.

Place the center of a protractor over the center dot of your circles. Mark off every 45 degrees with a little dot. Use a see-through perpendicular ruler to lightly draw lines dividing the circle into eight equal triangles by drawing through the protractor lines and the center dot of the circle.

Now the fun begins. The basic premise is that whatever you do on one side of the circle, you must balance it with the same thing on the opposite side.

It is important to remember that all new lines that you add to develop your design must begin and end at the intersection of a protractor line and a compass line. For example, if you want to create a long and rather thin pointed shape, you would begin on one of the intersections of a compass line and a protractor line that is close to the center of the circle.

You could connect to another intersection of a compass line and protractor line that is closer to the outer edges of the circle, and then return to a different compass/protractor intersection that is again nearer to the center. Then you would balance that on the opposite side. The same would hold for compass arcs. If you want to create a series of arcs in your design, place the center of the compass on an intersection and place your pencil in the compass on whatever compass/protractor intersection you wish, depending on how large you want your arc to be. Then swing your compass to make the arc. It's nice to drop back a bit and make parallel arcs in your design so that they might later be filled in as thicker, more dominant lines for variety of line width in your final design. (Or they could be filled in with checkers or patterns, stripes, etc.)   Parallel lines are a big part of developing the designs. Realize that every time you add a new part to your design, you have crossed over several or many of your original compass lines as you traverse your new line from the inner area of the circle to the outer edges, or vice versa. That means that each time you draw a new addition to your design, you have created many new intersections over the original compass lines. These new intersections then become additional possibilities for beginning and ending future additions to your design. Remember the rule that all new additions must begin and end on the intersection of one of your compass lines and a line that passes through it. The more you draw, the more intersections you create, the more possibilities there are for developing your design further.

Keep developing your design by repeating whatever you draw on one side of the circles to the other side. Watch as your design grows in complexity.

After you have developed your design with your balanced points, arcs, and parallel lines, you are ready to start adding patterns and filling in with pen or pencil. Add your patterns in such a way as to keep various line densities balanced in your total design. In other words, if you fill in one part of your design with a delicate pattern, the next part of your design that touches it should be filled in with something darker or a more tightly packed pattern. Develop areas of contrast.

You can also develop some of the original compass circles that are closely parallel to each other. Parts of these parallel circles can be filled in with step patterns, checkerboards, etc., to look as though they weave in and out of the points and arcs that you developed in your design.

When you are completely finished coloring, erase your pencil lines.

Allow your inner spirit to express itself onto paper.

Once your mandala is finished, put the date you completed it. You may want to note how long it took you—the number of hours or the number of days.

Hang your mandala on a wall or on your refrigerator where you can see it regularly. Each day spend a few minutes simply looking at it, and allow it to explain itself to you. As you get thoughts on its various meanings, write these observations down around your mandala. This is a nice way of remembering what emotions you were feeling or exploring at that time in your life.

Constructing a Mandala Using Sand

Materials needed:
Sand—it may be a nice idea to make your mandala on an outing to the beach.

Procedures:
Give yourself the time to create your mandala, perhaps an hour or so. You may want to put on your favorite music, but turn off your phone.

Before you begin, you may want to clarify the intention of your design or give a word of thanks to the universe. You also may want to request guidance and insight so it is your inner teacher who is creating your mandala. Use your intuition and allow a shape or color that comes to you to be reflected in your work.

Working with damp sand is most likely the best and easiest. You can add some dry sand as part of your design.

Begin at the center of the mandala and work outward. You can use your finger, a shell, or a small stone to etch a symmetrical design into the sand. You can use circles, spirals, or other geometrical shapes.

When you have finished, sit back and meditate on your mandala. Depending on the timing of the tides, see if you can sit long enough for the tide to come in and wash your mandala away.

Coloring Your Mandala

Coloring is perhaps one of childhood's greatest joys. As a child, coloring helps to express our early creativity. It helps us discover our inner expression. As an adult, we can still experience that same joy. Even if you do not consider yourself to be creative, your creativity will soar when working within a frame and allowing your instinct to decide on the colors you choose for your mandala. Do not feel obligated to follow any rules. It does not matter if colors in your mandala complement each other or not. It is your creation. In coloring you can find as much satisfaction, perhaps more, than if you created the outline of the mandala on your own. Just think of the possibilities of deciding the various hues of color to be placed next to each other, and how shading can affect the feeling a color emits. When we are able to create a unique and personal pattern and color scheme within a definitive framework, we are allowing our individuality to be in sync with the universe.

As you begin your mandala project, let your feelings and emotions guide you. Try not to think too much or determine what colors you should use. Statistically, even if a couple of hundred people colored the same mandala, no two would be exactly alike. Each mandala is a personal reflection of the individual who created it.

Start coloring your project where you would like. If you are feeling centered and grounded that day, you may begin your coloring at the hub or center point of your mandala and work outward. It could be a reflection of where you are right now, and where you want to go. Or you can begin from the outer edges and work inward. Sometimes when someone begins coloring from the outer edge, moving towards the center, he or she may find that a feeling of inner calm or inner awareness arises as their work progresses. Mandalas are concentration tools, so you should work in whatever way you feel most comfortable. There is no right or wrong way.

Once you complete your mandala, you may want to mark the date you finished your project for future reference. You also may want to jot down whether you created your mandala from the inside out or the outside in. You may observe a pattern or patterns in your creations that will give you insight into differing areas of your life and various emotions you are experiencing.

Follow your coloring project with one of the meditations described earlier in this book.

Mandalas Are for Everyone and All Ages

THE PLEASURE OF coloring and creating mandala artwork can be experienced by all regardless of age, occupation, or creative ability. Many times we feel that coloring and creating mandalas are only for children, or only for those with a religious background. Working with mandalas is a way for an individual to explore his or her inner being, even if the person knows nothing of the subject matter. The shapes, the symbols, and the colors involved are ways to visually express our deepest feelings and thoughts. Mandalas can be created by one person working on his or her own as an independent exercise, or in pairs or groups. It is a fun way for parents to relate to their children. Mandalas can be a means of play for children to discover their distinct attributes, and a way for couples or friends to get to know each other. So much can be revealed in a joyous, non-threatening way.

Mandalas are liberating adventures that allow our souls to experience new heights of insight through the beautiful realization of the connection and circle of life.